I LOVE OUR AIR

Carol Greene

Enslow Elementary, an imprint of Enslow Publishers, Inc.
Enslow Elementary® is a registered trademark of Enslow Publishers, Inc.

Original edition published as *Caring for Our Air* in 1991.

Library of Congress Cataloging-in-Publication Data

Greene, Carol.
    I love our air / by Carol Greene.
        p. cm. — (I love our Earth)
    Includes index.
    Summary: "Find out what air is, why it's important, and how people can protect it"— Provided by publisher.
    ISBN 978-0-7660-4037-3
    1. Air—Pollution—Juvenile literature. 2. Air—Juvenile literature. 3. Environmental protection—Juvenile literature. I. Title.
    TD883.13G743 2012
    628.5'3—dc23
                            2011023710

Future editions:
Paperback ISBN 978-1-4644-0140-4
ePUB ISBN 978-1-4645-1047-2
PDF ISBN 978-1-4646-1047-9

Printed in the United States of America

032012 Lake Book Manufacturing, Inc., Melrose Park, IL

10 9 8 7 6 5 4 3 2 1

To Our Readers: We have done our best to make sure all Internet Addresses in this book were active and appropriate when we went to press. However, the author and the publisher have no control over and assume no liability for the material available on those Internet sites or on other Web sites they may link to. Any comments or suggestions can be sent by e-mail to comments@enslow.com or to the address on the back cover.

Enslow Publishers, Inc., is committed to printing our books on recycled paper. The paper in every book contains 10% to 30% post-consumer waste (PCW). The cover board on the outside of each book contains 100% PCW. Our goal is to do our part to help young people and the environment too!

Photo Credits: Photos.com, p. 16; Photos.com: John Foxx, p. 7, Vladimir Ovchinnikov, pp. 4–5, 24, Wojciech Gajda, p. 19–20; Shutterstock.com, pp. 1, 3, 8, 11, 13, 15, 21 (crafts); Stockbyte/© 2011 Photos.com, a division of Getty Images. All rights reserved., p. 21 (boy).

Cover Photo: Shutterstock.com

Enslow Elementary
an imprint of

 Enslow Publishers, Inc.
40 Industrial Road
Box 398
Berkeley Heights, NJ 07922
USA
http://www.enslow.com

Contents

Air is all around us.
Every living thing
needs it to stay alive.

What Is It?

You can't see it. You can't smell or taste it. But you can't live without it.

What is it? Air.

Sometimes you can feel air moving past you. Moving air is called wind.

Sometimes you can see what air does. You can see it blow leaves on a tree or toss a kite in the sky.

Sometimes you can see other things in the air. You can see fog. It is made of tiny drops of water in the air.

Sometimes you can smell or taste things in the air. You can smell flowers. You can taste salt when you are near the sea.

But the drops of water, the smell of flowers, and the taste of salt are not part of air. They are just in it.

Air is made of gases such as oxygen, ozone, and carbon dioxide. It covers the whole earth like an invisible blanket.

We can see things that are blown by the wind, like these sailboats. But we cannot see air.

Why Is Air Important?

Air is important because all living things need it to stay alive. Without air, they die.

Different living things use different gases from the air.

When people and animals breathe, they take in oxygen. They give out carbon dioxide. Green plants and trees take in carbon dioxide. They give out oxygen.

This works well. It keeps the air right for all living things.

These raccoons give out carbon dioxide when they breathe. The trees where they live take in the carbon dioxide.

Air is also important because it helps keep the earth warm. The invisible blanket of air lets in sunlight. It keeps the sun's heat close to the earth.

Air is important because it protects the earth from some of the sun's rays. These rays can harm people's skin.

The gas called ozone stays high in the blanket, or layer, of air. It keeps some harmful rays from getting through.

The air protects us from some of the sun's rays. But it is also very important to use sunscreen.

What Can Happen to Air?

People can make air dirty by putting pollutants in it. Pollutants are harmful things left over after burning or making something.

Most pollutants come from burning things. We burn fuel in cars, trucks, and planes. Power companies burn fuel to make heat and light. Some factories make things by burning.

All of this burning puts pollutants in the air. Pollutants make the air hard to breathe. They can make people and animals sick. Pollutants can harm plants and trees. They can even harm buildings and bridges.

Some pollutants can kill. Once, a poisonous gas got in the air from a factory in India. It was an accident. But over 3,000 people died.

Factories release pollutants that can make the air unsafe.

Air does not stay in one place. It moves around. So dirty air from one state can hurt plants and trees in another state. Dirty air from one country can make people and animals sick in another country.

Sometimes there is too much carbon dioxide in the air. It can come from burning things. But it also comes from cutting down too many trees. The earth needs those trees to use carbon dioxide.

When there is too much carbon dioxide in the air, more of the sun's heat stays close to the earth. The earth gets too warm. Some people say this is happening now.

Sometimes pollutants float high into the air. They destroy the ozone there. Then harmful rays from the sun can get down to earth. Right now there is a hole in the ozone layer over the South Pole.

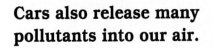

Cars also release many pollutants into our air.

Planting a tree is a good way to keep our air clean and healthy.

What Can We Do?

People can stop putting so many pollutants in the air. They can stop driving so much. They can find fuels that don't make pollutants. They can make better cars, trucks, and planes.

Factories can find cleaner ways to make things. They can find safer ways to get rid of pollutants. If people do these things, they will have cleaner air.

People can also stop cutting down so many trees. They can plant new trees. Then there won't be so much carbon dioxide in the air, and the earth won't get too warm.

People can stop putting pollutants into the air that destroy the ozone layer. Then the ozone layer will keep harmful rays away from the earth.

People can make laws for clean air, too. We already have laws for better cars and fuel. But people must make more laws like these.

Countries must work together on laws. Then everyone must obey the laws.

Keeping our air clean will cost money. It will take work. But clean air is worth it!

What Can You Do?

You can help keep air clean, too. Here are some things that you can do.

- Turn off lights, computers, and TVs when you are not using them. That will save fuel.

- Close doors behind you when you go in or out. That will keep warm (or cool) air inside and save fuel too.

- Walk or ride your bike. It's good for you, and you'll save more fuel.

- Plant a tree. It will use carbon dioxide. If you can't plant one by your home, see if you can in a nearby park, or at school.

- Talk to your family and friends about buying fewer things made of paper. Paper is made from trees and the earth needs those trees.

- Try to use recycled paper when you can.

Recycle paper.

Make your art projects from recycled materials.

Words to Know

air—A mix of gases that covers the earth.

carbon dioxide (KAR bun dy OX eyed)—One of the gases in air.

factory—A place where things are made.

fuel (FYOOL)—A substance that people burn to get heat or power.

gas—A substance without definite shape or size that floats freely, like oxygen.

oxygen (OX i jin)—One of the gases in air.

ozone layer—It protects the earth from the sun's harmful rays.

poisonous (POYZ un us)—Harmful to people, animals, and plants.

pollutant (poh LOOT ent)—A thing left over after burning or making something. It is harmful to the earth.

power—Energy used to do work, like light a house, or run a TV.

Learn More

Books

Jimenez, Nuria, and Empar Jimenez. *Blow! Air*. Hauppage, N.Y.: Barron's Educational Series, 2010.

O'Ryan, Ellie. *Easy to Be Green: Simple Activities You Can Do to Save the Earth*. New York: Simon & Schuster, 2009.

Royston, Angela. *Polluted Air*. Chicago: Heinemann-Raintree, 2008.

Threadgould, Tiffany. *ReMake It! Recycling Projects from the Stuff You Usually Scrap*. New York: Sterling, 2011.

Web Sites

EPA: Recycle City.
<http://www.epa.gov/recyclecity/>

Save the Earth for Kids.
<http://www.SaveTheEarthForKids.com>

Index